Herbs, Health and Astrology

Herbs, Health and Astrology

by   Leon Petulengro

Illustrated by Linda Diggins

Keats Publishing, Inc. ✖ New Canaan, Connecticut

Publisher's note: Wherever sugar is called for in recipes in this book, honey may be substituted in the same or less quantity, according to taste. Wine may require substantially less honey than sugar, but double the amount of beer yeast. (Beer yeast is *live* yeast; the brewer's yeast referred to in the recipes is the British term for live yeast used to make beer or wine, *not* the yeast killed by heat we know in the U.S.A. as 'brewer's yeast' and buy in health food stores as a food supplement.)

HERBS, HEALTH AND ASTROLOGY

Published in 1977 by Keats Publishing, Inc.
by arrangement with Darton, Longman and Todd, Ltd.
London, England

Copyright © 1977 by Leon Petulengro
All Rights Reserved

ISBN: 0-87983-148-0

Library of Congress Catalog Card Number 76-587-69

Printed in the United States of America

Keats Publishing, Inc.
36 Grove Street, New Canaan, Connecticut 06840

Contents

Introduction

The Rhythm of Life

It was my grandmother, Anyeta, from faraway Romania, who first introduced me to the mysteries of herbal remedies as the Romanies know them. Her wise, lined face would crinkle in a smile as she recited the qualities of her favourite herbs, lingering lovingly over their fragrance and texture, and ruminating on their ancient powers.

'Stand on any hill,' she would tell me, 'and look for miles around at the view. There will you see God's bounty growing, just for the taking ... plentiful. In everything that grows we find the mystery of life a million times.'

She was right, of course. Why there is such variety in life remains a complete and eternal mystery. Why a thousand species of insect? Why a million species of grasses? A billion kinds of green growing things? Why did not the eternal One grow just one 'herb' on his planet Earth – a green stuff like spinach – and say: 'That's your lot. Sufficient unto the day ...!'

Instead, we have this wonderful variety from which to choose, each green growing thing, from a humble grass trodden underfoot to a giant Redwood tree scraping the sky, with its own use in life, its place in nature, its history and background enough to fill a book.

And through all this abundant life there is a pulse beating which we Romanies and the wise ones of old – the astrologers – believe to be a rhythm which is generated in the universe. As the planets in their courses whirl and pulsate, so their rhythm is one with the herbs that grow on earth, all life that breathes, the tides that beat our shores.

If the scientists have gone a million miles towards knowing the secrets of this life, then by all means let us applaud them. But there is one way in which they could be deemed less wise than their predecessors – the alchemists who laid the groundwork for the chemists, the herbalists who went before the doctors, above all, the astrologers who led the way into astronomy (how many know today that the first Astronomer Royal, Flamsteed, was also an astrologer?). They have taken so long to acknowledge the rhythm of life that is everywhere and which is set down in the philosophy we call Astrology.

Now, however, it has been discovered, by scientific means, and recorded by the Nutritional Science Research Institute of England, that *each individual food or material or disease radiates energy of a radiation-type characteristic via a unique pattern or wave field. This is an extended force field that exists around all forms of matter, whether animate or inanimate.* So, knowing as we do that planets and stars emit their own individual signals or vibrations, how can we disbelieve that ancient lore was right and that herbs and plants, and indeed humans, are ruled by these various vibrations or force fields. The cosmic influence at last seems to be acknowledged by the white-coated men of science. What better time than now, on the threshold of the New Aquarian age, to re-examine those ancient beliefs of the Wise Men and admit that they were not uttering mumbo-jumbo – but were infinitely wise before their time.

Culpeper, the seventeenth century astrologer and herbalist, believed this to be the true philosophy of life. He not only assigned each herb its ruling planet, but treated each subject of the Zodiac – the hot-headed Arien, the stubborn Taurean, the mercurial Geminian – according to their lights, their planets, their 'stars'.

His advice to the readers of his *Complete Herbal* on when to gather herbs for treatment was as follows: 'Such as are astrologers (and indeed none else are fit to make physicians) such I advise; let the planet that governs the herb be angular, and the stronger the better; if they can, in herbs of Saturn, let Saturn be in the ascendant; in the herbs of Mars, let Mars be in the Mid-heaven, for in those houses they delight; let the Moon apply to them by good aspect, and let her not be in the houses of her enemies; if you cannot well stay till she apply them, let her apply to a planet of the same triplicity; if you cannot wait that time neither, let her be with a fixed star of their nature.'

To anyone with an ear for English that passage reads like poetry; to an astrologer it also contains precise instructions, as does the following advice from Culpeper on *'The way of mixing Medicines according to the cause of the Disease, and part of the body afflicted':* 'To such as study astrology (who are the only men I know that are fit to study physic, physic, without astrology, being like a lamp without oil) you are the men I exceedingly respect, and such documents as my brain can give you at present, being absent from my study, I shall give you.

1. Fortify the body with herbs of the nature of the Lord of the Ascendant, 'tis no matter whether he be a Fortune or Infortunate in this case.

2. Let your medicine be something anti-pathetical to the Lord of the Sixth.

3. Let your medicine be something of the nature of his sign Ascending.

4. If the Lord of the Tenth be strong, make use of his medicines.

5. If this cannot well be, make use of the medicines of the Light of Time.

6. Be sure always to fortify the grieved part of the body by sympathetical remedies.

7. Regard the heart, keep that upon the wheels, because the sun is the foundation of life, and therefore those universal remedies Aarum Potabile, and the Philosopher's stone cure all diseases by fortifying the heart.'

Whether this early form of treatment stands up against modern medicine with all its 'advanced' drugs, is not my argument here, but let us admit it sounds more enchanting to the philosophical ear than 'Keep on taking the tablets'. As

I have said so often before, a man who will not give some credence to astrology, will damn it before he knows anything of its methods, its history or traditions, has no poetry in his soul, to say the least. My main purpose here is to record some of the ancient, beautiful beliefs about the herbs which grow around us, and their link with astrology. If, in doing so, I interest you and entertain you and make you begin to think about alternative ways to 'be', other ways to think, different rhythms to adopt in your life, then I have satisfied myself that this little book has served a marvellous purpose.

For, as my ancestor, Jasper Petulengro, once said in Borrow's Lavengro: 'Life is sweet, brother ...' But the knowing of that sweetness, the learning of it, needs a special effort on the part of many a modern human being, trapped in the concrete landscape of city life. To walk on grass, breathe sweet air, has become something of a privilege, almost an impossible dream to millions of us. Many, of course, do not want or need such an existence, having been horribly conditioned by now to the diesel-poison of polluted air, the hard, springless arid waste of city sidewalks. If only they knew, if only they could know, what pleasure is to be had from regaining knowledge of old country lore, of cooking with herbs, eating them fresh in salads, using them for gentle medicaments against ill health, instead of rushing to the harsher, faster methods of modern science.

If only ... then they would rediscover a most pleasant land – the land of tranquillity, of the rhythm of life as my people once knew it.

The secret is everywhere ... perhaps you will make a start by reading this book and learning about the riches that our ancient herbal lore has to offer in this computer age.

May I wish you *kooshti sante* – good health in mind and body, and a long and happy life.

Leon Petulengro

ARIES

(The Ram)

(MARCH 21st – APRIL 20th)

Element: Fire   *Planet: Mars*

Among the people born under the Sun sign of Aries are the leaders and pioneers of this world. Always on the go, anxious to get things done, the average Aries man or woman cannot bear the thought of being unoccupied; in this lies their strength and also their weakness, for although in modern terms they could be called the great 'achievers' they create their own dangers. Quick tempered, they usually like to 'have things out'; if they cannot they could be subject to conditions such as high blood pressure or migraine, both a result of stress or frustration. Nervous types suffer from hay fever, asthma – at least, that is how the Arien sometimes expresses his inner anxiety.

It is a basic rule of health for any Aries man or woman to try to take things calmly and ignore minor irritations. The lesson to be learnt is to let others share the work, learn to delegate; the typical Aries subject tends to believe that only he is capable of doing what is desirable or essential in any work situation.

Ariens should concentrate on a mainly vegetarian diet – especially onions, tomatoes, spinach – should not take alcohol or smoke. The driving force of Mars gives them a tough constitution, but a tendency to push their potential to the limit, and the result could be permanent ill health. There is an alternative – good health from following the rules of astrology.

Health points to watch: nerves, head, blood pressure, sinuses.

Herbs for health: Rosemary, Marjoram, Garlic, Horseradish, Cowslip.

ROSEMARY
Rosemarinus officinalis

Ruled by Sun in Aries

Let's look at Rosemary, that most delightful herb, and my favourite, first. Rosemary or 'dew of the sea' is a herb that was said to grow more abundantly and fragrantly in this country than anywhere else on earth and to be at its most fragrant by the sea. Of it Culpeper, in his wisdom, has said: 'It helps weak memory and quickens the senses. It is very comfortable to the stomach in all the cold maladies thereof; helps . . . the digestion, the decoction of powder being taken in wine . . .' This decoction was also said to help rheums of the eyes and other cold diseases of the head and brain, the head being the area of the body most afflicted in the Aries healthscope.

Some of the legends which surround this herb are of a sacred nature, some more mundane. Here are two contrasting legends. It was said that during the flight into Egypt the Virgin Mary threw her robe over a rosemary bush while she rested beside it and for ever afterwards the delicate white flowers turned to blue.

Have you ever heard the old saying, 'Where rosemary grows, Missus is Master'? I have no proof that it is true, but my people always held that rosemary was a guard against evil spirits, and a future bride would slip a sprig of it under her pillow before her wedding night.

If you want to grow this bushy herb in a pot remember to keep pinching out the growing points and it will stay a sensible size; otherwise, left to its own devices in sandy soil rosemary will grow to a height of five feet in open ground, but it looks best against brick or stone, as Sir Thomas More knew, for he let it 'runne all over my garden walls'.

It has a very strong aroma that comes through well in any potpourri, and it makes the best of all hair lotions. My mother, who prided herself on her abundant locks, used this recipe: Take a few sprays of the fresh or a dessertspoonful of the dried herb, cover with water, simmer for fifteen minutes or more, allow to cool, strain and use as a rinse.

In cooking, rosemary is traditionally used in this country with pork or lamb roasts or beef stew. In Italy it is used with veal and in veal stuffing. It was also once used with hare or leveret and in olden days was distilled with Molasses spirit to make Hungary water.

Have you tried adding a spoonful of chopped rosemary to your scone or biscuit mixture? It imparts a very distinctive flavour and though it may not be to your taste, it is worth trying once. And if you need a helpful bedtime drink for feverish colds try two parts chopped rosemary to one part lavender, infused as a tea.

Added to the bathwater it makes a delicate and soothing remedy for aches and pains; my grandmother would fill a muslin bag with the herb – it lasted several sessions. And a few sprigs in a jug of boiling water is a good remedy for a tired complexion – you just hold your face over the steam after the herb has been infused a few moments and let it warm and rejuvenate your skin.

SWEET MARJORAM   Ruled by Mercury in Aries
  Origanum marjorana

Culpeper said it was an excellent remedy for the brain and other parts of the body. Also: 'The powder snuffed up into the nose provokes sneezing, and thereby purges the brain; chewed in the mouth, it draws forth much phlegm.'

This is a particularly fragrant and pleasant herb; it's an ingredient of bouquet garni and is used in cooking to flavour many meats.

Sweet marjoram is best grown as an annual, sown out of doors in April and thinned to nine inches apart. Pot marjoram is a perennial and can be propagated by division or seeds in April.

A handful of the fresh herb, taken after it has been infused in boiling water, is a good cure for a headache, to which Aries people are singularly prone.

A hotter mediterranean version of marjoram is oregano, also called 'joy of the mountains'. The Italians use it in pizzas and it is especially pungent sprinkled over grilled tomatoes. It is included in the making of anchovy paste.

GARLIC
Allium sativum

Ruled by Mars

Culpeper said that garlic 'Wonderfully opens the lungs, and gives relief in asthma; nor is it without its uses in wind colic'! The mediaeval doctors believed it had many uses and would carry a clove of garlic in their bags as a combined cure and guard against evil spirits. The herb was probably introduced into Europe by the crusaders, having been known in the Middle East since the beginnings of civilisation, where it was not only believed to be a good digestive but a powerful magic too. It certainly has a powerful smell, and if one's mate is not a garlic fan there can be terrible consequences! The trick, said my father, Xavier, who loved it, is to chew a few cummin seeds and the odour will be overcome. People tend to be entirely for or against the herb – there are no 'don't knows'.

HORSERADISH
Amoracea rusticana

Ruled by Mars

This fiery-tasting root has been used as a medicament since early times. Give some thought to whether it's wise to plant it in your garden, for once it takes a hold, you may well be hounded by the herb; it will grow everywhere. Its link with the Arien is that it is ruled by Mars – its elemental fire appeals; and it's also in tune with the Arien's desire for fierce remedies – it's a powerful antiseptic, and not a gentle herb at all.

In cooking it is used mainly with beef as a sauce or cream, but it is also delightful with roast chicken, fresh water trout, and the Swedish countryfolk make it into a sauce combined with puréed apples and white wine.

COWSLIP
Primula veris

Ruled by Venus in Aries

The Greeks had a name for it. They called the humble

cowslip *paralysis* because of the qualities of the little yellow flower which remedied palsies and cured trembling. My father used to tell of how an old countryman said to him when he was a child that if he dug up a primrose and planted it upside down then a cowslip would grow from the root. His experiments were always failures. But when he grew older he learnt to make a good cowslip beer, which if taken in too great a quantity certainly helped him to see things upside down!

Here's the recipe: You need a fairly large barrel into which you put four-and-a-half gallons of light ale. Have ready half-a-bushel of cowslip flowers picked from their stalks and add these to the beer, close down the bung and leave for a fortnight. At the end of that time strain off and bottle, adding a lump of sugar to each bottle.

Cowslip wine is particularly delicious and can be drunk as an aperitif; it soothes the nerves and induces sleep and is very good for feverish colds.

My father's recipe: *Boil 3lb loaf sugar in 4 quarts water for ½ hour, skimming carefully. Put into a big pan the grated rind of 2 oranges and 1 lemon with the juice of all 3. When the sugar water is quite boiling pour it into the pan, stirring well. Allow to get cool, but not quite cold, then add 4 quarts of cowslip flowers that you have picked from the stalks. Also ¼ oz compressed yeast, moistened with a little water; 2 tablespoons brewer's yeast is better. Stir thoroughly, cover with a cloth, and let it stand untouched for 48 hours. Then turn it into a clean cask, bung closely and leave for 2 months. (Some people add ½ pint brandy when the wine is put into the cask, but this is not necessary). Draw off, strain and bottle after 2 months and store in a cool place.*

TAURUS
(The Bull)

(APRIL 21st – MAY 22nd)

Element: Earth   *Planet: Venus*

This sign of the bull symbolises beauty and fertility. Taureans are rather 'earthbound', stubborn; they stand with their feet firmly planted on the earth and are not easily persuaded against their will. The commonest complaints afflicting Taurus people derive from wrong diet – they tend to like sweet and rich foods and to put on weight in middle life. Sugar, especially starchy pastries and cakes should be avoided at all costs. Taureans who neglect exercise and diet will regret it in later years.

Health points to watch: the neck, throat, gullet, larynx, vocal chords, digestion.

Taureans should eat plenty of fruit, apples, blackberries, gooseberries, peaches; and for vegetables – beans, peas, spinach, potatoes, carrots and celeriac.

Herbs for health: Mint, Thyme, Tansy, Coltsfoot, Lovage.

GARDEN MINT   Ruled by Venus
  Mentha viridis

Everyone surely knows and loves the clean fresh smell of mint straight from the garden, although one is startled to learn from Culpeper that he considered mint juice taken in vinegar 'stirs up venery, or bodily lust'. It is, after all, a herb of Venus. He also recommended it for the more mundane disorders of the stomach, such as 'weakness, squeamishness, loss of appetite, pain and vomiting'.

First brought to Britain by the Romans, mint thrives here

in rich, damp soil. If you find it tends to wander, then plant it in a pot below ground to confine the roots.

An infusion of mint is helpful in cases of skin trouble, and the fresh leaves laid against the skin help to dispel headaches. Use mint freely not only with lamb, as mint sauce, but to sprinkle on carrots, beetroot, boiled potatoes and peas. It combines well in salads and especially in fruit salads.

In olden days mint was used to scent baths, as a dental wash, and was said to keep away both flies and mice! Today it is used as a delicate and refreshing cosmetic; it is easily obtainable in the form of oil and you should combine it with oils of lavender, jasmine, roses and lemon to obtain a delicious scent for your bath.

There are so many ways to use mint that I could not possibly list them here, but my mother used it in our Romany vardo to prevent the churn of milk from curdling, and made a wonderful mint and apple jam, as well as mint jellies, juleps and chutney. Here is her recipe: *Wash some cooking apples, cut them in halves, peel and core them. Put them into a pan 3 parts covered with cold water, bring to the boil and simmer till tender. Rub through sieve, add a large bunch of fresh mint and $\frac{3}{4}$lb sugar to each pint of the apple pulp and cook, stirring, until the jam sets. Then take out the mint and pot the jam.*

She also used to make a delicious mint and parsley butter, by combining the mint and parsley leaves (no stalks) in equal quantities, boiling them gently until soft and then rubbing through a sieve. The purée was then mixed into a quarter of a pound of butter until smooth, with a dash of cayenne.

Peppermint tea is especially helpful for digestive upsets, or as a pick me up, and is refreshing instead of coffee after dinner. Just infuse the whole leaves like ordinary tea and if you want a really health-giving drink, add a few chamomile flowers to the mixture.

For that lovely drink mint julep, which is so reminiscent of the warm South of the United States on a summer day, you'll need some fresh mint leaves, three teaspoons of sugar syrup per glass (equal quantities of sugar and water), one ounce of whisky per glass, crushed ice and a sprig of mint for decorating. Put the ice in the glass first, add sugar syrup, whisky and mint leaves, stir, bruising the mint. Fill the glass up with broken ice, then add another dash of whisky and stick a sprig of mint on top. Don't serve until the glass is frosted.

THYME   Ruled by Venus
Thyme vulgaris

Once again the Romans are responsible for introducing to our wild northern shores this lovely little herb from the warmer climes of the Mediterranean. The delicate smell of thyme is a joy on a sunny day. Romany girls place sprigs under their pillows to drive away nightmares. A tough little herb, it is also the emblem of courage, for its name is said to be derived from the Greek *thymos*.

I expect you know the grey, bushy garden thyme from the green-leaved lemon scented thyme. The bees, said to be the wisest beings in nature, have always loved this herb and honey made from thyme is certainly ambrosia. My father kept bees once he had stopped his travels and always planted thyme near his hives.

It grows easily on light, sandy, or chalky soil and can also be cultivated on heavier, but not moist soil.

It is one of the three herbs used in a *bouquet garni*, it is one of the oldest herbs to be used in the kitchen, and has a pungent strong flavour that is easily recognisable.

Mediaeval herbalists used thyme-vinegar for headaches, and thyme tea for curing flatulence and stomach troubles. My mother used to make a tasty thyme stuffing for poultry: *4 oz white breadcrumbs, 2 oz butter, 1 tablespoon chopped onion, salt and pepper, 1 tablespoon thyme and parsley, grated rind and juice of a lemon and 2 tablespoons yoghurt or soured cream. Fry the onion, mix the ingredients all in a bowl and bind with the sour cream, or yoghurt.*

Of course, the most soothing mouth rinse of all is glycerine of thymol if you have a troublesome throat – which Taureans so often find is their weak spot. Thyme combined with lavender and chamomile makes a soothing vapour treatment for a tired skin (Taurean women always pride themselves on their beautiful skins) and thyme used in a herb pillow adds a distinctive scent to the whole – say of lavender, lemon verbena, tarragon, sweet woodruff, marjoram and hops.

TANSY   Ruled by Venus
Tanacetum vulgare

The common Tansy is a dear little plant. Culpeper says 'the same boiled in vinegar, with honey and alum, and gargled in the mouth, eases the tooth-ache, fastens loose teeth, helps the gums that are sore, settles the palate of the mouth to its place, when it has fallen down!' which is a surprising thing to learn.

The little flowers are yellow, the taste of the herb bitter and aromatic, too strong for some people, but tansy puddings made from the garden variety used to be common in rural parts of England, and Easter tansy pudding is still eaten in Yorkshire; it was also taken to counteract the effect of overeating, which Taureans may note!

If you'd like the traditional recipe for tansy pudding, here it is. Most people today would think it a bitter and curious dish: *3 oz white breadcrumbs, ½ pint milk. Heat milk and pour over crumbs. Beat up 2 eggs with an ounce of sugar and 2 teaspoons of finely chopped tansy leaves. Mix with the breadcrumbs and ½ oz butter and bake in a pie dish. It should be eaten cold, with cream.*

COLTSFOOT   Ruled by Venus
Tussilago farfara

The brave little yellow flowers blossom and die before the leaves appear, and these stand straight by the roadside like little soldiers, braving the cold winter to herald spring in February. Syrup made from the plant, or juices were a favourite cough remedy or expectorant in olden days, and in many parts of the country it is indeed called *coughwort*. The Latin *Tussilago* is taken from *tussis*, 'cough'. My father's remedy for coughs was to put a handful of leaves into a quart of water and simmer till reduced to a pint, strain and pour while hot into a jug with a slice of lemon. Sweeten with honey. A wineglassful is the dose to be taken three or four times a day.

Coltsfoot is the foundation of most herbal smoking mixtures. My father made his tobacco of equal parts of eyebright, buckbean, betony, rosemary, thyme, lavender and camomile flowers, dried and chopped fine, then added to an amount of coltsfoot equal to the rest.

My grandmother has a recipe for threadveins which she gave to fair skinned women. (This is something most Taurus women suffer from as time goes by, for their skins are delicate.) She would pat warm milk on the face, allow to dry for ten minutes, then wash it off with cool water. She made coltsfoot compresses by infusing one tablespoon of coltsfoot flowers in a cup of cold milk, or a cup of boiling water (the milk takes several hours – the boiling water infusion takes fifteen minutes) then she wrapped the herbs in a gauze napkin and laid the compress against the affected area.

LOVAGE   Ruled by Sun in Taurus
Ligusticum levisticum

This classic herb has a traditional reputation as a natural deodorant and has, as far as I can tell, no powers as a love potion, which some people suppose. There is, however, the legend that country girls of Bohemia used to carry lovage in small muslin bags hanging round their necks when they went to meet their lovers.

Lovage has luxuriant foliage, and emits an aroma very like celery; like celery, the stalks are suitable for blanching and can be eaten raw with salt; the leaves can be used in salads, or herb sauces. But the part most used medicinally is the root, and ancient herbalists reckoned that 'the distilled water of lovage cleareth the sight and putteth away all spots, lentils, freckles and redness of the face, if they be often washed therewith'. There is no doubt that it is one of nature's antibiotics.

The distilled water was said to help quinsy in the throat

and made a good gargle; it was also used as an eye lotion.

My grandmother occasionally used lovage in her washing water; she boiled the root for half an hour, strained the water for use, with a few drops of oil of spike and a little musk as fixative.

If you would like this perennial from the mediterranean shores in your garden you will find it grows to a height of three or four feet in fairly rich soil. The seeds can be sown in spring or autumn, or the plant increased by division of the roots. It needs plenty of moisture.

GEMINI

(The Twins)

(MAY 23rd – JUNE 21st)

Element: Air   *Planet: Mercury*

The mercurial processes of the mind of a typical Gemini are the by-products of a quick metabolism! The Gemini man or girl is restless, entertaining, sometimes intellectual, always alert. Gemini people have their antennae working all the time, receptive to sensations of sound and sight and even, sometimes, ESP. Needless to say, total nervous exhaustion is their main trouble. So, if you're Gemini, watch your nerves; try to get times alone to be tranquil. The Zodiac decrees a weakness of the lungs, shoulders and arms – all dual organs or limbs, you will note, for this dual sign.

Your quicksilver temperament needs calming and soothing and it is very important that you get enough sleep.

Meat is not good for Gemini people, who need the vast array of minerals and organic salts in fresh fruit and vegetables to keep them feeling healthy; tomatoes are good, beans, bean sprouts, mushrooms, carrots, watercress and asparagus, sweetcorn. For fruits: apricots, peaches, plums, figs and mulberries.

Gemini subjects are sometimes prone to catarrhal attacks and should take little or no cows' milk. Goat's cheese is best for them.

Health points to watch: shoulders, arms, lungs, nerves, mucous linings.
Herbs for health: Parsley, Lavender, Dill, Caraway, Mulberries.

PARSLEY

Apium petroselinum

Ruled by Mercury

Parsley is surely the best-known household herb of all. Parsley sauce, parsley potatoes, parsley and lemon stuffing – we all have our favourite ways of using it in the kitchen and I can think of nothing more fragrant than the scent of fresh parsley added to a stew.

My father used to have some parsley every day, either fresh or dried, for, he swore, it was the best herb for settling his stomach!

Modern researchers have found that parsley is a herb rich in vitamins A, B, and C, that it is anti-flatulent, anti-spasmodic and anti-fermentative, and that it stimulates the digestive glands and improves the working of the whole digestive tract. The herbalists of old were very well aware of these properties.

A herb originally from the Eastern Mediterranean, its legendary background springs from the classical age. According to Greek mythology it grew from the blood of a Greek hero, Archemorus, the forerunner of death. As a symbol of strength it was used to adorn the brave.

If you want to cultivate parsley you will have to be patient! The seeds take from four to six weeks to germinate (six times to the Devil and back!) and my grandmother used to say that 'parsley would only grow if it liked the sower'! So, if parsley is unfriendly to you, better to be content with buying it in the shops. It does not object to shade and you can grow it in a window box easily.

Did you know that the Romanies always maintained that if you sowed your parsley seeds on Good Friday, health and happiness would be yours that year?

It's a hardy biennial which needs rich, well-worked soil so the roots can go deep, and, as I've said, it loves to hide in the shade. Sow twice a year, in April and July.

Here's a tip for speeding the germination – soak the seeds in water for twelve hours prior to sowing. In the second year the umbels show a profusion of florets, green-yellow, and then there's an abundance of seeds which will be ripe by the end of September and will keep fertile for nearly five years.

So many of you must be familiar with a dozen good recipes for parsley that it would be a waste to give any of the more common here, but for those who like parsley potatoes, there's this tip. I remember my mother used to roll the potatoes first in a mixture of lemon juice and a little melted butter, then mixed in the finely chopped parsley.

Parsley jelly was one of my favourites as a child. It used to be served with cold chicken or ham: *Fill a saucepan with the leaves of the herb and add cold water – just enough to cover them. Bring to the boil and then simmer for $\frac{1}{2}$ hour. Measure the liquid, add the juice of 1 lemon and its rind for every pint. Strain again and allow 1 lb lump sugar to each pint of the liquid. Boil until the jelly sets and pot. Leave to cool and then cover.*

LAVENDER
Lavandula officinalis

Ruled by Mercury

Of all the scents of summer, nothing is more specially English than the wafting fragrance of the lavender bush, growing in its favourite place by a shady wall, set about by the flagstones of a cool terrace, mixed with the scent of June roses, perhaps. Shakespeare called it 'hot lavender' because of its particularly warming scent. Culpeper said the oil 'is of a fierce and piercing quality, a very few drops being sufficient for inward or outward maladies'.

Lavender was one of the herbs my grandmother especially loved. She enclosed the dried flowers in sachets to sell from door to door; she was hooked on it herself and always kept a scented bag in her linen chest in the vardo. She used lavender oil and lavender water to keep insects away in the summer.

Anyeta also used lavender as part of a mixture for infusion as a herbal facial steam – which I believe is now becoming very fashionable as a beauty treatment once more. She would place two handfuls of mixed dried herbs in a bowl, fill with hot water and then hold a large towel over her head and over the bowl and let the steam refresh her skin. This was the mixture: sage leaves, chamomile flowers, lime flowers, lavender flowers, nasturtium flowers, nettle leaves. She, like my mother, often used a little oil of lavender in a footbath of warm water to relieve aching feet.

One of the Gemini traits is talkativeness, though always in an entertaining and passionate manner; one could never say that the Gemini is a bore! Culpeper said: 'Two spoonfuls of the distilled water of the flowers help them that have lost their voice, the tremblings and passions of the heart, and fainting, and swoonings, applied to the temples or nostrils, to be smelt unto, but it is not safe to use it where the body is replete with blood and humours because of the hot and subtle spirit wherewith it is possessed.'

My mother's remedy for nervousness was always to put a spot of lavender water on a lump of sugar and suck it! She made her lavender water at home. Here is her recipe: *1 lump of sugar, 3 drops oil of lavender (or oil of spike) 1 pint clear distilled water. Put the oil on to the sugarlump, place in a bottle with the distilled water and shake vigorously. Cork, leave aside for 1 week, and it will be ready.*

Another trick of my mother's was to put two or three heads of lavender in the sugar bowl (yes, we had sugar bought from the local village store, my father having developed a sweet tooth) and it was scented in a delicious manner.

DILL   Ruled by Mercury
Anethum graveolens

This is a herb which is rich, aromatic and pungent. Its name is said to derive from the ancient Norse, *dilla*, meaning to 'lull' a baby, and it is, indeed the main ingredient of gripe water, which was once used to lull babies into a more tranquil mood.

The seeds are used more than the plant, and in olden times people often chewed dill seeds during the fast before church service, so as to stay their hunger pangs.

It is a good herb for the digestion, and brings a hot spicy pungency to rather watery foods. Cucumber, tasteless and rather indigestible, is pickled with dill to make it more tasty and more digestible.

Sow your dill seeds in the spring after the frosts have gone, and thin the plants out to a space of a foot or more (they grow to about three foot in height). Germination takes twenty to twenty-eight days. The flowering time is from July to August and the seeds can be gathered in September. They keep their fertility for two to three years.

Dill is very rich in minerals and the Romany girls of years ago ate the herb a great deal when pregnant because of its reputation for stimulating the milk in nursing mothers. Modern researchers have discovered this to be true, and have also found that dill is a pleasant flavouring for people on a low salt diet because of their high blood pressure – it contains salts that are easy on the system.

The traditional uses of dill in this country are many and varied: on canapés, and in fish spreads; the chopped leaves can be used in salads – potato, tomato – and go well in cream cheese. The seeds can be used in dressings, in pancakes or omelettes, in vegetable or chicken soups, with trout, mackerel, on grilled steaks, roast chicken, in fish sauces, and in cucumber sandwiches in place of salt.

I remember my mother's method of making dill potatoes went like this: *Boil and slice some peeled potatoes (about 3 lb), sauté a finely chopped onion in margarine or corn oil, add 2 oz flour to the onion mixture and some cold water to make a roux, then slowly add ½ pint stock, salt, pepper, and 2 tablespoons green or dried dill, freshly chopped, add the potatoes and bring to the boil, then reduce to a simmering heat. Lastly, stir in some sour cream or yoghurt – about 7 tablespoons.*

Fried fish is often improved by dill sauce. Make it this way: *Take 1½ cups white sauce, 1 large dill cucumber, sliced, 1 dessertspoon sherry and 1 dessertspoon (level) dill seed. Mix the sherry in the heated white sauce, add sliced cucumber and dill seed. You serve it hot.*

CARAWAY
Carum carvi

A herb whose hot breath is known in this country best when you take a slice of traditional seed cake! As a child it always brought tears to my eyes! But Culpeper noted that 'the root is better food than parsnips; it is pleasant and comfortable to the stomach, and helpeth digestion'.

It is believed that the name *carum* is derived from Caris, a district in Asia Minor which is particularly rich in aromatic herbs.

Sow it in your garden in August. Germination takes twenty to thirty days. When the plants come up, thin to one foot apart. The young green leaves may be used, finely chopped, in salads. The new growth, next spring, will be a single stem of about one and a half feet. Seeds should be gathered before they fall in late summer, dried off and used in cakes, bread, cheeses and cabbage dishes. Caraway seeds remain fertile for two years.

Seed tea is probably not anything you have ever tasted or ever expected to sample, but should you have problems with wind after meals or digestive pains then try this remedy!

Take a small quantity of caraway seeds, fennel seeds and anise seeds in equal parts and crush with a pestle. Pour boiling water over the crushed seeds and allow to stand for fifteen minutes or more when strained, this is a very pleasant drink with warming qualities.

MULBERRY
Morus nigra

Ruled by Mercury

Surely everyone who can remember a childhood in the country knows the mulberry tree. The purple juice of the berries is delicious and has wonderful healing qualities. There is no part of the tree that ancient herbalists did not use. The berries were used to cure coughs, inflammations or sores in the mouth or throat, and the bark and leaves, when used as a decoction, made a good mouthwash. The bark of the root, said Culpeper, 'kills the broad worms in the belly'.

My mother's personal remedy for 'chestiness' was a simple

mulberry jam which, though rather runny, was delicious. Stew the berries in a saucepan without any water, to extract the juice. Add enough honey to make a thick syrup after the juice has been strained.

My father preferred mulberry wine: *7 lb mulberries stripped from their stalks, 3 gallons water. Put the berries in a pan and pour over the water, boiling. Leave for 2 days, bruise and strain through a jelly bag. Measure the amount of liquid, and to each gallon add 3 lb loaf sugar, 1 lb unstoned raisins, $\frac{1}{4}$ oz ground ginger, 6 cloves. Put into a pan and boil gently for 1 hour, skimming when necessary. Draw from the heat, and let stand until nearly cold, then stir in brewer's yeast in the proportion of 1 teaspoon to each gallon. Turn into a dry cask, cover the bunghole with a cloth and leave for a fortnight. Add a wineglassful of brandy to each gallon, bung down tightly and leave for 6 months, then bottle and cork.*

CANCER

(The Crab)

(JUNE 22nd – JULY 22nd)

Element: Water   *Planet: The Moon*

Cancer people are emotional, being of the element Water, and their moods wax and wane as rapidly as the Moon on its progress through the Zodiac each month. They can easily suffer from digestive upsets and should eat well-cooked food and take time over meals. They benefit from eating fish, living near the sea and cultivating a tranquil atmosphere.

Always try, Cancer, to overcome your tendency to worry. The diet that suits you best is of fresh fruits and salads, white and shell fish, plenty of milk, cheese and raisins. You could lack calcium, so that dairy products are helpful, and all kinds of cabbage, kale and onions, too. Other valuable foods are oranges, lemons, parsley, chives, leeks.

Health points to watch: stomach disorders, liver, nerves, varicose veins, eye trouble.
Herbs for health: Agrimony, Balm, Daisies, Lettuce, Cucumber.

AGRIMONY   Ruled by Jupiter in Cancer
Agrimonia eupatoria

The common agrimony grows in ditches and in the borders of fields and along the hedgerows and is a small plant with green and grey hairy leaves, and small yellow flowers. It has been used for hundreds of years as a mild astringent, tonic, diuretic. My father recommended one ounce of the dried herb being infused in one pint of boiling water, sweetened and then taken in small doses for coughs, or diarrhoea. Culpeper found that 'it openeth and cleaneth the liver, helpeth the jaundice and is very beneficial to the bowels ...'.

The name is thought to have originated from the Greek *argemos* for 'cataract' and eye disease, and indeed down the ages distilled water of agrimony has been used for an eye lotion.

BALM   Ruled by Jupiter in Cancer
Melissa officinalis

The delightful lemon-scented herb balm with its bright green heart-shaped leaves is a bright spot in any garden. As soon as the tiny white flowers are open they are the centre of attention from the bees, and indeed the Latin name *Melissa* means Bee. It was supposed to be used as one of the sacred herbs in the temple of Diana, and in more recent times bee keepers used to rub beehives with balm to keep the swarm together and attract newcomers.

In cookery balm is used mainly to flavour soups, stews, sauces and dressings and can be used to flavour salads and cool drinks; it also makes a cooling tea. My mother made balm tea by pouring one pint of boiling water upon one ounce of the herb and letting it stand for a quarter-of-an-hour to cool. Then she strained it before drinking.

Culpeper recommended that a syrup be made of the herb to give comfort to out-of-sorts stomachs. It was also said, taken in wine, to be a remedy against the bite of the scorpion or of a mad dog!

If you would like balm in your garden you can grow this little shrubby perennial in any soil. It can be sown in May, or you can take cuttings or division of the roots in the spring and autumn, but not later than October. Seeds should be sown in the greenhouse, then pricked out two inches apart in a seed box when they are an inch high. When four inches high, transplant into the garden at about eight inches to a foot apart. The plants die down in winter but grow green again early in spring.

DAISIES
Bellis minor perennis

Ruled by Venus in Cancer

Nobody who has ever made a daisy chain has not got these little wild flowers engraved upon the heart; the bright golden eye is a cheerful sun with pure white rays. The fleshy green leaves lie flat to the ground. Pretty they are by name and by nature, and we would suppose that Bellis is taken from the Latin *bella*, but the plant's power as a wound herb was well known, as we learn from the ancients, so perhaps the name comes from the Latin *bellum*, for 'war'. Whatever the truth, the English name is taken from the Anglo-Saxon 'daeges-eage', meaning eye of day, because it opens and closes its flowers with daylight.

The Romany girls used to make use of the juice of the daisy stalk for clearing blemishes from their skin; to cure a blotchy skin an infusion of daisy heads left on the face until it dries is another remedy from Romany lore.

LETTUCE
Lactuca sativa

Ruled by the Moon

After the hop the lettuce is one of the best of our home remedies against sleeplessness; eat lettuce (without vinegar) for supper and I assure you that you will have sweet dreams. It also soothes pain and is very mildly laxative. Lettuce tea, made by boiling a leaf or two in half a pint of water for twenty minutes is a remedy against constipation; drink the tea hot before going to bed.

The lettuce is a cooling and calming little plant, in fact the Emperor Augustus thought that his recovery from a severe illness was due to lettuce and built an altar and a statue in its honour.

CUCUMBER
Cucumis sativus

Ruled by the Moon

My mother's favourite remedy for freckles! Her fair skin was always powdered with gold in summer and she vowed that she had great success from her natural packs of sliced cucumber placed all over her face; she could feel the astringent qualities working, too, as she lay still. Not the least of the virtues of this process was to make her rest, for she was always on the move!

Today you can use the blender to extract the juice, or juices if you mix with pure lemon juice and witch hazel. Take out of the blender and add beaten egg white, pat on the face and allow to dry, wipe off with cool water and dab dry.

Modern research into the cucumber reveals that it contains 40 per cent of Potassium, 15 per cent of Sodium, 8 per cent of Silica, 7 per cent of Calcium and 7 per cent of Sulphur and is wonderfully cleansing to all blood and skin conditions. It also contains a hormone which is an anti-wrinkle aid.

LEO

(The Lion)

(JULY 23rd – AUGUST 22nd)

Element: Fire   *Planet: Sun*

How these vital and fiery people love to live – and live a long time they will! Back trouble is their natural weakness – the long spine of the lion – and muscular pain is common in this area. Rest whenever possible to avoid undue strain on the heart, Leo, learn to take it easy – although perhaps you will not need to learn, for some members of this Zodiac Sign are like the lazy lion after a meal.

But how their enemies do fear them when they attack – so high-blood pressure is a point to be watched!

Leos should eat cabbage, eggs, oranges, plums, peas, asparagus, coconut, nuts, raisins. They should avoid too much red meat, and take their protein in cheese, chicken, lentils.

Health points to watch: back, weak circulation, over-exertion, heart.
Herbs for health: Bay Leaves, Borage, Rue, Chamomile, Saffron.

BAY TREE   Ruled by Sun in Leo
  Laurus nobilis

The noble bay tree is a common sight in a Mediterranean countryside where its origins are in legend. The brows of the victorious were adorned with it as a symbol of the sun. It grows to about twenty feet or more. The leaves can be used in cooking either fresh or dried, and who has not watched their mother put a bay leaf in rice pudding? At least, mine did. Here we use the leaf with fish, meat, game, root vegetables, cauliflower soup and, as a sixteenth century medic said: 'when they are casten in the frye they crake wonderfully'. Physicians of old used bay berries' oil to relieve pains of the joints, nerves and arteries and it was said to help in cases of convulsions, cramp and numbness. The oil was also used to cure ear-ache, and was said to take away the bruises of the skin from falls.

Whenever we were parked near the sea and fishermen sold their wares to us cheaply my father would buy up small herrings and souse them, or marinate them in vinegar. Putting a bay leaf inside each herring once they were cleaned and sprinkled with salt and pepper, he'd place them in a baking dish and nearly cover them with vinegar and some brown sugar. Then he'd tie paper over the dish and cook them in a slow oven until the bones were soft. They made a fine cold supper dish and the bay fragrance was distinct.

If you buy a bay tree in a pot make sure it has some protection from wind and frost and is in a sunny position for much of the year. The leaves can be picked all year round but you can easily dry them for use at any time. They must be dried in the dark in fine layers and should be pressed under something heavy and flat and packed into airtight tins or bottles, not bags.

BORAGE   Ruled by Jupiter in Leo
Borago officinalis

There is an age-old legend that borage – that pretty, garden herb with its five-pointed starry flowers of Madonna Blue – made people merry and glad. I assume that I am correct in supposing that the legend had nothing to do with the effect of a Pimm's Number One. Alas, this is the only role in which most of us see this valuable herb today.

Herbalists have long used borage as a medicine for the heart and circulation. A compress with a solution of borage was said to relieve congested veins after long hours of being on one's feet, and my grandmother swore that it prevented varicose veins. Indeed, borage does seem to have an effect on the heart in that it stimulates it, makes it feel easy, keeps you feeling awake and lively.

Borage is a member of the forget-me-not family. It is an easily grown annual, the seeds being sown in April and thinned to twelve inches apart when the young plant appears. The leaves can be used in refreshing fruit drinks, cider or claret cup, to which it imparts a light cucumber flavour; they can be chopped up in salads, and the flowers can be candied for cake decoration.

Here is a seventeenth-century recipe for the candied borage flowers: 'Boil sugar and rose-water a little, then put the flowers thoroughly dry, with the sugar, and boil them a little; then strew the powder of double-refined sugar upon them, and turne them, and let them boil a little longer, taking the dish from the fire; then strew more powdered sugar on the contrary side of the flowers. They will dry themselves in two or three hours on a hot sunny day, though they lie not in the sunne.'

And here's an excellent recipe for a Leo who feels lazy and doesn't want to face the tasks ahead – have a cuppa borage tea! You can use fresh or dried leaves – and you can add the flowers for good measure – my mother called it 'the cup that cheers' all right – no wonder country folk call it the 'Herb of Gladness'.

RUE   Ruled by the Sun in Leo
Ruta graveolens

Garden rue, the Herb of Grace, or Herbygrass, or Ave-grace, as it was known, was a highly valued medicinal herb. Mediaevals believed that it was a strong medicament against the bites of scorpions and bees, hornets and wasps and that the smell of burning branches of rue would frighten away serpents.

In my father's day rue was called 'The Poor Man's Heal All'; there was no ill under the sun it was not warranted to heal, but he used it in only two ways. The bruised green leaves he laid on any part of the body troubled by sciatica. It often worked when all else had failed to relieve the pain.

And rue tea was used to cure dizziness or hysteria in women. When I was a child I knew a farmer's wife who fed rue to her poultry, for she found that her hens flourished when the herb was occasionally mixed with their meal.

This shrubby plant has a very strong smell and you may not appreciate it in your garden, but it is certainly of decorative value – a hardy evergreen that grows from eighteen inches to two feet high. It will flourish in poor soil but likes a sheltered position. You can propagate it by division of the roots, but you can also use cuttings, or sow seed in early spring.

CHAMOMILE   Ruled by Sun
   Anthemis nobilis
CHAMOMILE
   Matricaria chamomilla known as German Chamomile

The Ancient Egyptians dedicated this herb to the sun because, they said it cured agues. 'And,' says Culpeper, 'they were like enough to do it, for they were the arrantest apes in their religion I ever read of.' In spite of this insult he does not contradict the dedication and so one assumes he agreed that chamomile was ruled by the sun.

My mother used a rinse of flowers of the true chamomile (Matricaria Chamomilla) on her golden hair and then dried it naturally in the wind or the sun – and of course she always washed it in rain-water, by the way. Anyeta liked to drink tea made of the little yellow flowers, for it soothed her if she happened to be feeling cross about something – though I once saw her add a tot of brandy which did nothing to help the properties of the tea, I am sure.

Besides being a hair lightener, chamomile is a softening agent, so that it would pay anyone with sensitive, fine, fair hair to make a strong infusion of the flowers (fresh or dried) and add it to their rinsing water. And anyone with an oily complexion should make a natural astringent of yarrow and chamomile in equal parts – strain off, bottle and keep in a cool place– and then after you have cleaned the skin every morning, pat on the lotion. An infusion from the flowers also makes a very soothing compress for tired or red eyes, when sprinkled on pads of lint or cotton wool.

SAFFRON
Ruled by the Sun in Leo

Crocus sativus

It's appropriate, surely, that this fiery, golden yellow herb should be under the jurisdiction of the sun. The famous saffron powder, which gives the square yellow cakes from Cornwall their name, is gathered and dried from the three golden middle pistils of the deep mauve flowers which bloom in September.

Saffron Walden in Essex, a town I knew well as a child, is named after the herb, because huge quantities used to be grown there commercially, and it has three saffron flowers included in its coat of arms in honour of the herb.

Now, I was born in Spain (my father at that time being on a long and sunny journey with my mother, for he had been commissioned to buy up quantities of oranges for Tiptree, the famous jam-makers) but I was too young to remember the use of saffron in the famous *paiella* – a traditional dish of rice with mussels, squid, fish and crustaceans and chicken. However, I always remember my father raving about it. My mother used the herb in chicken soup, and it very much enhanced the flavour.

Saffron is an expensive herb, almost as scarce as gold dust, because it takes over two hundred thousand pistils to make one pound of the powder, but it is needed only in very small quantities in cooking – indeed, Culpeper cautioned his readers against taking too much of the herb as a medicament, for it produced sleepiness and he warned that 'some have fallen into an immoderate convulsive laughter which ended in death'. However, he recommended it to cure fainting fits, and palpitations of the heart, diseases of the lungs, hysteria in women, stomach disorders, smallpox and measles!

Saffron was, of course, a much used dye, and the Bible tells us that the clothes of the Children of Israel were bright and gay and dyed with saffron for yellow, madder root for red and the murex snail for purple. In mediaeval times saffron was used as a hair dye and here is the recipe: Mix equal parts of elder bark, flowers of broom and saffron, plus the beaten yolk of one egg boiled in water. Skim off the *pomade* that floats to the surface and use as a dye for the hair. (The effect is reddish rather than silver blonde.)

If you want to sample saffron, try using it with your favourite recipe for dumplings in the next meat or chicken stew. Just sift the dry ingredients, heat the milk and a pinch of saffron together and mix to a firm dough.

VIRGO
(The Virgin)

(AUGUST 23rd – SEPTEMBER 22nd)

Element : Earth   *Planet : Mercury*

Virgo subjects act quietly under a veil of reserve, appearing placid and cool when inwardly they are nervous. Virgoans tend to worry because they are perfectionists, both about themselves and about other people. They should lead a calm, natural life with plenty of fresh air and ignore their latest worry with the motto – 'Well, I have done my best and that is good enough.'

Virgo people often suffer from a shortage of Potassium Sulphate; this is to be found in celery, tomatoes, red beet, lemons, apples, parsnips, chicory. Figs, dates and hazel nuts are also health giving.

Health points to watch: nerves, abdomen, intestines.
Herbs for health: Fennel, Savory, Southernwood, Valerian.

FENNEL   Ruled by Mercury
   Arethum foeniculum
        'Above the lowly plants it towers
        The Fennel with its yellow flowers.'

So says Longfellow and so it is. For the magnificent, beautiful fennel with its feathery golden flowers, is a herb to be reckoned with – a strong plant with a strong flavour and not at all for the weak hearted. The legend has it that Prometheus and Epimetheus his brother, finding that man, whom they had created on earth, was left without gifts – for all had been given to the animals – ascended to Heaven and concealed in a hollow fennel stalk the fire of the sun in order to bring it down to man as the most powerful gift of all.

The Romans were responsible for the spread of fennel from the Mediterranean shores – in Rome their gladiators sprinkled it over their food to give them courage – through Northern Europe; and although it does prefer to occupy a sunny position it will grow good-naturally in any soil.

Fennel has always been regarded as one of the best remedies to aid the digestion, and has wonderful carminative properties. It is also calming to the nerves – the ideal herb for a Virgoan, who so often has digestive trouble or a nervy disposition.

It's also a nursery herb, for in olden days the midwife would wash the eyes of the new-born with fennel water. Culpeper says that the 'leaves, or rather the seeds, boiled in water, stays the hiccough'. The seed was also said to be good for stopping wheezings.

A perennial, capable of reaching a height of five to eight feet, the herb is best grown from seed sown in March or April and thinned to eighteen to twenty-four inches apart.

In the Middle Ages fennel was used to make salt fish palatable; it is indeed often referred to as 'the fish herb', and is especially good with herring, mackerel and salmon. The young leaves and stems can be chopped up and eaten in salads, or boiled as a vegetable and served with butter.

To make a fennel sauce my mother added chopped fennel to her basic white sauce, but she did not let the sauce boil after the fennel was added. You can also make mayonnaise suitable for cold fish such as salmon by adding chopped fennel, and the herb goes particularly well with scrambled eggs – just add a little of the chopped leaves to the eggs before cooking.

SAVORY   Ruled by Mercury
Summer – *Satureia hortensis:* Winter – *Satureia montana*

Savory was said by the Romanies to be good for taking away the pain of a bee sting and Anyeta, I well remember, used this method once on me.

There are two varieties: Summer savory is a low growing annual, sown in April and thinned to six inches apart. Winter savory is a perennial, shrubby plant, growing about one foot high. Both make excellent little hedges for a herb garden. Summer and Winter are similar in flavour and can be used in stuffings, fish and egg dishes or boiled with broad or runner beans. A little added to home-made tomato sauce gives a nice tang. It is a very pungent herb with a slightly peppery, aromatic flavour.

My mother's method of making savory stuffing for lamb was this: *Combine chopped onion with soft breadcrumbs (about 4 oz) 4 teaspoons fresh or 2 teaspoons dried savory, a little butter, plus about 7 crushed juniper berries, salt and pepper. For fish she left out the juniper berries, of course, and added an egg and some lemon juice.*

SOUTHERNWOOD   Ruled by Mercury
Artemisia abrotanum

My father used to make a hair tonic of southernwood and swear it prevented baldness. I do not think he stayed around long enough to discover whether his predictions came true for any of his male customers. That's the advantage of being what you might call a travellin' man.

The powdered herb can be made into a tea which should be brushed into the roots of the hair and left to dry, should you wish to test his theory.

Ancient herbalists used the herb to cure hysteria, and to cure ague and inflammations of the eyes. Boiled with barley-meal it removes pimples, said Culpeper, and we learn too, that he shared my father's view in that 'the ashes mingled with old salad oil, helps those that are bald, causing the hair to grow again on the head and beard'.

The flowers of the southernwood are small and yellow.

VALERIAN   Ruled by Mercury
Valeriana officinalis

The name is probably derived from the Latin *valere* 'to be

healthy', my father told me. For a Romany he knew a great deal of Latin, especially the Latin names of herbs and flowers. He thought valerian to be the strongest little herb when it came to inducing sleep and always used it as a night-cap when he found sleep elusive. The herb was also known to the Greeks as a calmer of nerves, so perhaps it is especially effective in the Virgoan 'healthscope'.

You can get valerian today as tablets, which have no side effects, or you can take it as tea, but I do warn you that the smell is not pleasant. My father's method was an infusion of one ounce of the root, to one pint of boiling water, taken in doses by the wineglassful. Derbyshire people know the herb well, for it grows in great quantity there, its small white flowers blooming in June and July. The root is the part most used in medicines.

LIBRA

(The Scales)

(SEPTEMBER 23rd – OCTOBER 22nd)

Element: Air   *Planet: Venus*

Libran subjects should do everything in moderation! One of their greatest temptations is the lure of good living, and they sometimes tend to suffer from kidney trouble in middle life. Because of this they should always drink plenty of fresh cold water.

Although theirs is the Sign of Balance, they have a way of being indecisive to a degree about questions large and small and such dithering is not good for the nerves, theirs or anyone else's who happens to be in the vicinity. They need a great deal of sleep. Who was it said 'six hours for a man, seven for a woman and eight for a fool'? Well, Librans are not fools, but they are always healthiest if they have a good night's rest.

Sun-Librans should eat celery, apples, spinach, radishes, strawberries, pomegranate, beans, corn, raisins and almonds. *Health points to watch:* kidneys, lumbar regions, skin, nerves. *Herbs for health:* Dandelion, Yarrow, Penny Royal, Violet.

DANDELION   Ruled by Jupiter in Libra
Leontodon taraxacum

Parney-kip-lulagi was my father's Romany version of the lion-hearted wild flower which grows riotously in these isles. Or, as the French would say, the *piss en lit*, 'vulgarly called Piss a Beds', says Culpeper.

Great minds with but a single thought, for this is one of the best of diuretics of nature and is a wonderful herb for the typical Libran. Everyone is familiar with the golden flowers, which can be made into a wonderful wine, and some know the peppery taste of fresh dandelion leaves in salad, with their serrated edges from which comes the name 'dents de lion' – teeth of the lion. But how many of you have tasted dandelion coffee, made from the dried roots? It's a marvellously soothing drink after a meal and contains no caffeine (which is so bad for the heart) and is remedial for gout, rheumatism and dyspepsia.

Dandelion juice is the Romany cure for warts. Squeeze a leaf or flower and a drop of milky-looking juice will appear at the broken end. Touch the wart with it and leave the liquid to dry on. Repeat as often as you can and soon the wart will turn black and then leave the skin, unmarked, for ever. My father had a conviction that warts were caused by touching the water in which an egg has been boiled – he rated it a first-class poison!

His dandelion wine, however, was far from poisonous. Here's his recipe: *Gather 2 quarts dandelion flowers, petals only, put them into a big pan, and pour over them 2 quarts of absolutely boiling water. Cover with a clean cloth and leave for 3 days, stirring as often as convenient. Strain the liquor into a preserving pan, with the thinly pared rind of 1 orange and 1 lemon, 2 lb loaf sugar, a piece of whole ginger about an inch in length, and the lemon, cut into slices. Boil for ½ an hour. Put it back into the pan and allow it to get cool, though not cold. Spread ½ a tablespoon of brewer's yeast or 1 oz compressed yeast on a slice of toast and add to the wine. Leave for 2 days, pour into a cask and keep it well bunged down for 2 months. At the end of that time bottle for use.*

YARROW   Ruled by Venus
Achillea millefolium

Country folk know the white flowers of Yarrow by other names: Nose Bleed, Millfoil and Thousand Leaf (both the last are references to the Latin, *millefolium*). But the name yarrow is taken from the Anglo-Saxon *gearwe* which seems to have belonged once to vervain, when it signified 'holy'. *Achillea* is in honour of the Greek hero Achilles who is said to have used the plant to cure wounds received by Telephus, son of Hercules.

As a beautifier yarrow has astringent qualities, and an infusion, cooled and used on the skin of the face would have great effect on oily skin with open pores. Four tablespoons of yarrow soaked in two cups of milk for four hours and used as a wash will prevent blackheads. And if you have oily hair, then make yarrow your friend; drink the tea several times a day and add the infusion to your rinsing water. Anyeta used to say a yarrow footbath was the most soothing thing for sore or calloused feet.

My father recommended an infusion of one ounce to one pint of boiling water to be taken in wineglassfuls, drunk with the chill off, and he would add a teaspoonful of Composition Essence to every dose. He combined yarrow with elder flowers and peppermint as an influenza cure, for it is diaphoretic, stimulant and tonic.

The internal benefits of yarrow are many – it is a diuretic, helps rheumatic pains, and is helpful in cases of liver and gallbladder. My mother always served a yarrow salad in the summer months when the white flowers starred the hedgerows. For this she combined cucumber, chopped yarrow flowers, watercress, chives, mixed with chopped cold boiled potato and a lemon dressing.

PENNY ROYAL   Ruled by Venus
Mentha pulegium

Penny Royal runs along the ground, its slender stalks bearing their tiny purple flowers shooting up from the lateral growth at intervals.

Its country name is from the early Latin name *Puleium regium*; written in some herbals as *puliol royal*, which we could translate as 'a sovereign killer of fleas'. Pulegium is indeed derived from the Latin *pulex* 'flea', but although Culpeper described it as a herb that would cure most things from jaundice and dropsy to whooping cough, he made no mention of fleas, unless you count the information that a decoction 'helps the itch'.

The Greek legend surrounding penny royal is that it is named after a nymph, Minthe, (Mentha) daughter of Cocytus, who was turned into a plant of mint by Persephone in a fit of jealousy.

It has a warming effect, like most mints, and is good for curing flatulence.

I give my father's recipe here for mint water as a cure for flatulence. He used any kind of mint from peppermint to garden mint or penny royal: *Put 1 lb loaf sugar into a quart jug and add enough boiling water to nearly fill. Stir frequently till the sugar is all dissolved. Then add sixpennyworth of essence of mint to be bought from any chemist and, if it is proposed to keep the cordial for some time, a wine glassful of gin. This latter can be done without if preferred. Without it the cordial will remain good for some weeks. Pour all into bottles and cork tightly. Dose: a wineglassful whenever the digestion is troublesome. It is also good for colds.*

VIOLET   Ruled by Venus
Viola odorata

The beautiful Sweet Violet, with its dark green leaves which hug the earth and look so cool, and its lovely little blue flower, holds a secret. It has antiseptic properties which are not yet fully understood or investigated.

Herbalists used the violet for easing head pains, for cooling burns and for purging the body of poisons. It was said to help the quinsy, epilepsy in children, pleurisy, diseases of the lungs, and bladder pains. The leaves, infused and strained were used once in 1902 to 'cure a case of cancer of the throat', and when asked about this my father said that he firmly believed it was so, for he had heard country people tell tales of banishing growths by use of this recipe.

You pour a pint of boiling water on a handful of fresh violet leaves and leave to stand for twelve hours. When required the water is strained and applied to the affected part on lint. Another case of 'cancer' was reported as cured through the patient drinking one pint of infusion of violet leaves. But it is certainly not a remedy that works in every case or in every type of cancer, for if that were so, we should long ago have rid ourselves of the terrible disease.

Violet syrup was used when I was young as a cough syrup and violets used as an infusion make an effective eye treatment for inflamed lids or sore eyes. A mixture my father used was an eighth of a teaspoon each of dried fennel, eyebright, chamomile and violet in a cup of boiling water, which is allowed to cool and applied on lint compresses.

SCORPIO

(The Scorpion)

(OCTOBER 23rd – NOVEMBER 21st)

Element : Water   *Planet : Mars*

The magnetic Scorpio is a mystery to most people; secretive, deep, a mass of extremes and contradictions. Scorpio people have amazing powers of tenacity and resistance, so that when they are ill they often recover quickly through sheer will power! Their main disadvantage is that they are always at war with themselves – for they know their own weaknesses and, being at the root humanitarians and moralists, they find it difficult to cope with the darker side of their nature.

They have a very long life expectancy, yet they can be their own worst enemies – drinking and smoking to excess or eating too much animal fat, for they have to watch their heart and circulation and all these things are dangers to them. Their other problem is complications of the urinary and reproductory organs. Despite this, they are decidedly strong in constitution.

Scorpions should avoid excess in anything, should eat fruit and green vegetables, watercress, cabbage, kale, prunes, onions, liver and avoid salty things like bacon, sausages, pork, etc. They should eat black cherries, oranges, lemons, asparagus, rhubarb.

Health points to watch: heart, circulation, urinary tract and reproduction organs.
Herbs for health: Basil, Nettles, Tarragon, Barberry.

BASIL   Ruled by Mars in Scorpio
Ocimum basilicum

Basil is a truly delicious herb when used in cooking and if you have never tried it, I advise you to do so soon, for it goes well in soups, stews, sauces and is especially fine, as the Italians know, with tomatoes.

There are two kinds – Sweet Basil and Bush Basil and it is Sweet Basil we are concerned with here. The herb comes originally from India, and does not take at first to our colder climate, so that it should be sown under glass in March and kept there till the frosts have gone and then the seedlings should be transplanted about nine inches apart. If the weather is fine you can sow outside in May in a sheltered place. The herb grows to a height of two or three feet.

Sadly, basil is not used a great deal in British kitchens, and could do with a revival. Its aroma is distinctive and its flavour clove-like; a sprig is sometimes included in a *bouquet garni*.

My father said that an infusion of basil, taken last thing at night, would stop a cold in the early stages. And one of the best ways of making vinegar palatable to anyone with a poor digestion is to bruise some fresh leaves of basil, fill a glass jar with them, loosely packed, then fill up with good wine vinegar, cover and leave in a cool place for a fortnight. Pour the liquid off through a strainer and re-bottle.

My mother's version of tomato sauce for lamb always included a little chopped basil, as well as onion, carrot, celery, thyme and parsley. She'd simmer the lot (two pounds of ripe tomatoes as well, naturally) for longer than an hour, then rub the purée through a sieve. But if you haven't that much time, why not try a little chopped basil with some parsley on your halved tomatoes when next you fry them.

The medicinal properties of basil are many and varied. It has been used as a sedative, against gastric spasms, as a laxative, a carminative and expectorant; it was also said to stimulate milk in nursing mothers.

It's a mystery to me why basil is surrounded with such off-putting folk lore — such as the way the Romans maltreated it when they planted it, trampling all over the ground and uttering curses! And the fate of Keats's Isabella and her pot of basil could be another legendary tale that discourages the faint-hearted. It's certainly a pity if the linking of basil with bad luck has made it scarce in our homes. But as a Romany I say – don't believe any of it. I think it is a wonderfully versatile herb and deserves a right royal place in your herb garden.

NETTLES   Ruled by Mars
Urtica dioica

Well, here it comes. My father actually grew his own bed of nettles! If you don't believe me I must go on to explain why.

This, the common stinging nettle, seemed to him of all nature's remedies to be of most value. In the spring and summer he ate boiled nettles, at least twice a week and he also used to make a decoction which he would bottle for use through the winter. For throat and chest complaints he boiled the nettles without salt, saved the water, added enough honey to make a syrup, and used it as a medicine. He also used the water externally for healing sores or abscesses.

Now the relevance to Scorpio is this – that nettle juice contains a magic formula for those with high blood pressure.

The stinging nettle that you as children are taught to avoid can be your salvation in adult life, for it is also rich in iron, is extremely alkaline and a solvent of uric acid, so that if taken regularly it will help to keep you clear of rheumatism. As for me, as a child I was taught to look upon young nettles as a valuable crop rather than a weed or a nuisance, and harvested them in spring by the sackful for sale to the local herbalist or chemist. I have never despised them because I know too much about them and their place in the history of herbs.

Country lore is full of praise for the nettle. Nettles yielded one of the best vegetable fibres for textiles, and in many parts of the country it was highly valued as a substitute for flax when a housewife had her own spinning wheel.

Make friends with the nettle. All you need is a pair of gloves!

TARRAGON

Ruled by Mars

Artemisia dracunculus

Tarragon has a delicate and subtle flavour of which the French make full use. Unfortunately, it is not such a popular herb in our kitchens. Tarragon is carminative, a source of warmth, and its sharp, sweet, scent gives piquancy to salads and to all cooked vegetables. Perhaps you are most familiar with tarragon vinegar, having seen it in the shops – but you can easily make your own with the fresh herb, once you have grown this lovely plant in your garden.

It's a perennial whose woody stems divide into many branches; the leaves are long and spear shaped and in July and August the little greenish flowers appear. It will grow to about eighteen inches in a sheltered position; the roots are very strong and are easily divided for propagation. If you want to dry the leaves, cut them before the flowers develop, and again in September.

To make tarragon vinegar, pick some leaves on a dry day before the flowers bloom, strip them from the stem and fill a glass jar loosely with them. Fill up the jar with wine vinegar, leave covered for some days and then, if after testing it you find it's already taken on the herb's fragrance, strain the vinegar through muslin, cork and bottle. You can use the dried herb in the same way – one heaped tablespoon of dried leaves to a pint of vinegar.

Tarragon is a herb much used for sauces. The French use it in the classic Sauce Tartare and in Bearnaise Sauce, but the quickest and easiest way to take advantage of its aromatic flavour is to chop up the leaves and boil them for a few minutes in a little water, then mix them with half a pint of white sauce, season to taste and serve. This is lovely with chicken.

Of course, tarragon is a true herb of *haute cuisine*, is known in all the best kitchens, and has a classic background – the Latin name is derived from the legend that the herb was dedicated to the Goddess of Nature, Artemisia, the twin sister of Apollo. But we Romanies were more familiar with its less illustrious relatives, wormwood, southernwood, cudweed and mugwort, all of which are artemisias. Southernwood, as I have already said, was used mainly as a hair tonic; bittersweet in scent and flavour, it was a common sight in herb gardens and in my grandmother's day and she knew it as Lad's Love. Mugwort was a favourite herb in mediaeval days for women's disorders. Cudweed was recommended as long ago as Pliny's day as a remedy for 'mumps and quinsies', and wormwood is used in the making of that famous French drink Absinthe.

BARBERRY   Ruled by Mars
Berberis vulgaris

Because my people are descended from the Berbers, the fierce, fair-skinned wanderers of North Africa, it is interesting to me to know that the common and genetic names of this little bush are derived from the Arabian name for the plant, *berberys* – plant of the Berber's'.

In herbal medicine its uses are tonic, purgative and antiseptic. The root, root-bark, or berries are used in cases of jaundice, liver complaints, general debility and biliousness. Its effect on digestive problems is due to the bitter alkaloid, Berberine, which has been isolated by modern researchers.

My mother made barberry jam from the berries by allowing equal quantities of the fruit to preserving sugar. She'd bring fruit and sugar to the boil very slowly then simmer for about twenty minutes, stirring and removing scum all the time. Then she would bottle the jam, covered closely. And she made a pleasant and refreshing drink from the berries by adding a fistful to a jug of boiling water, adding sugar to taste and stirring. When the liquid was cold it could be strained off and then used diluted with water as much as you would orangeade. With ice and soda it makes a much healthier and more life-giving drink than claret cup or any alcohol.

And if you think you're getting a cold and are feeling depressed, with the usual aches and pains, then barberry juice, made from the stewed, strained berries, taken hot and sweet last thing at night, will encourage perspiration and drive out the pain.

Nicholas Culpeper
17th century herbalist and astrologer

The secret is everywhere . . .
make a start by learning about the riches that
our ancient herbal lore has to offer

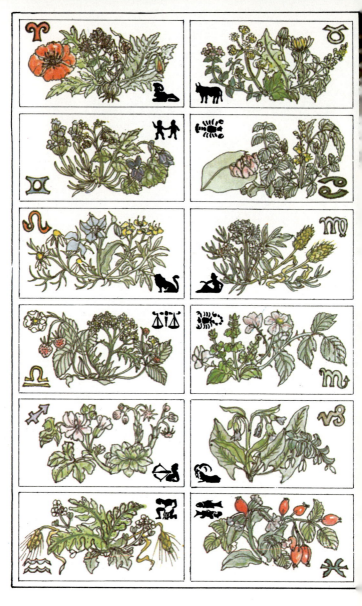

The signs of the zodiac and their related herbs

SAGITTARIUS

(The Archer)

(NOVEMBER 22nd – DECEMBER 22nd)

Element: Fire   *Planet: Jupiter*

Sagittarians are usually cheerful and philosophical, but rather restless. They enjoy being on the move and benefit greatly from the outdoor life. As long as the Sagittarian keeps the blood in good order, good health will follow. However, he does tend to have a hot temper, and when that's aroused it takes some time for tranquillity to prevail once more!

This Sign of Fire should beware of rheumatism, injuries to the hips or thighs and arterial problems. Sagittarians should eat lots of onions, parsnips, oats, asparagus, red cabbage, chicory, corn, barley, endive, cucumber, cherries, prunes, apples, but take very little red meat. White fish is also good for them.

Health points to watch: arteries, thighs, hips, joints.
Herbs for health: Sage, Samphire, Houseleek, Chervil.

SAGE   Ruled by Jupiter
Salvia officinalis

Surely everyone knows this little shrubby plant to be found in most cottage gardens. 'Jupiter claims this', says Culpeper, and so it is a herb for all good Sagittarians, like myself.

From times immemorial sage has been a famous herb. 'How can a man die who has sage in his garden?' asked the Arabs, and indeed its Latin name *Salvia* is derived from *salvare* to heal, or save. The Chinese held sage, not a herb of the Far East, in high esteem and traded it with the Dutch in exchange for their tea.

The evergreen woody shrub, which comes from the Mediterranean, likes plenty of sun, can be grown from seed sown in March (under protection) or from heeled cuttings in April, and will reach a height of about three feet.

My ancestor, Jasper Petulengro, highly appreciated sage and ate some every day to dispel the wind and improve his memory, so he told his wife, a strange dual role! It is good for the digestion, too.

Sage prefers a limey soil, but is not too fussy and will settle anywhere dry and heathy. There are several different varieties but the one with silver-grey leaves and little purple flowers is the herb most used in this country.

My people always rubbed a joint of meat with sage before roasting it, and one of the most delicious spreads you can make is four teaspoons of fresh sage and some lemon juice to four ounces of cream cheese. My grandmother made tea of the herb for anyone with an upset stomach, but she mixed the herb with a little lemon balm to make it less bitter to taste.

Sage and onion stuffing is a famous accompaniment to poultry, pork and lamb, but I always think it is improved by the addition of some chopped parsley. And, of course, that Romany standby, baked rabbit, was always served in our caravan with sage and onion stuffing, made from the herbs out of the garden of the local farmer's wife. (Gladly given to my mother by this lady, I may add, not stolen.) Sage fritters are very tasty, and I remember having them often as a child. Just add some chopped sage to your usual batter.

Sage has a beautifying role in our lives, too. For years my father gave advice to countrywomen on how to darken their greying hair. His counsel was to apply sage tea. 'Put a good handful of good garden sage, either dry or fresh, into a jug and cover with half a pint of boiling water. Add a teaspoonful of borax and allow it to get cold. To use, damp a brush or sponge in the tea and apply it lightly to the hair.' This is also an excellent hair tonic.

Sage was always used by the Romanies as a mouth cleaner and it is still used today by many Arab people. Just rub the leaves over the teeth and gums. A sage infusion, passed on to the skin of the face is also a good astringent for oily skin and open pores, and can be used to cool a sunburn.

What more can I say about sage, that king of herbs? It is a disinfectant, is a remedy against colds, coughs, stimulates the circulation and digestive tract, will help in cases of cystitis, rheumatism, depression, giddiness; is warm and comforting, and is said to aid the memory! Some sage every day keeps the doctor away, said my father to me – and I've heeded his advice ever since.

SAMPHIRE   Ruled by Jupiter
    Rock or small *Crithmum maritimum*

How marvellous it was as a child to accompany my father on his samphire searches among the rocks of the Suffolk shore. I remember on dry days – when the wind was blowing in from the sea, and the gulls circled loudly – scrambling over the slippery rocks looking in all the crannies for the little herb which grows around our Norfolk and Suffolk coastline, and is also to be found off the shore of South Wales.

My mother used to chop it up in soups, or serve it as a green vegetable, boiled with a pat of butter on it, and it had a distinct, rather bitter flavour, which I loved. The herb was also pickled: *Boil some vinegar with salt and peppercorns – ¼ teaspoon of salt and 4 peppercorns to each ½ pint. Allow to cool. Pour the cold spiced vinegar over the chopped-up samphire and then bottle.*

Samphire is said to be a corruption of St Peter's Herb – *Herba di San Pietro* – then *sampetra*, then *samphire* over the years. But I have never been able to find out why this herb was dedicated to St Peter, unless it was because he was a fisherman.

Ancient herbalists thought the herb fine for aiding the digestion of meats and for dissolving stone and gravel. I knew nothing of this as I sat in our Romany vardo relishing the samphire that we had gathered that day. I loved it and it's something which I sorely miss today.

Listen to Culpeper's description, which is poetic:

'It grows up with a tender green stalk about a half yard or two feet high at the most, branching forth almost from the bottom, and stored with sundry thick and almost round leaves, of a deep green colour, sometimes two together, and sometimes more on a stalk, sappy, and of a pleasant hot and spicy taste. At the tops of the stalks and branches stand umbels of white flowers, and after them come the seed larger than fennel-seed, but somewhat like it. The root is great, white, and long, continuing for many years; and is of a hot and spicy taste likewise. It grows on rocks that are washed by sea-water.'

I assure my readers that a great delicacy has been forgotten by the world – but if you are lucky enough to find some samphire (it's still sold in King's Lynn market), try it for your health's sake.

HOUSELEEK   Ruled by Jupiter
Sempervivum tectorum

Here is another marvellous herb, familiar to me in childhood, which grows on the roofs of country houses. In the days when cottages were thatched, the houseleek was encouraged rather than not, because it was believed to be a charm against fire, lightning and, incidentally, witchcraft.

The common name means 'house plant', the last part of the name is derived from the Anglo-Saxon *leac*, for plant. Country folk also knew it by the name 'Welcome-home-husband-however-drunk-you-be', perhaps an allusion to the leaning flowering stems. The Latin name is from *semper*, 'always', and *vivo*, 'alive', and the specific name *tectorum* is, of course, 'of roofs'.

You must have seen houseleek even if you did not recognise it for what it is – each plant has a circle of thick, succulent leaves, with a long stalk, and from this grow the starry flowers of red petals round a green dome which flower in July. The dome is the pod which holds the tiny seeds.

My father used a decoction of houseleek to cure fevers and chesty colds, shingles, and its effects even in the most serious of cases, were miraculous. Either the larger plant or the small houseleek (Sedum Minus) can be used for these purposes. These have small white five-petalled flowers. The root is fibrous.

The plant's juice, if squeezed on a corn or wart, will quickly removed the trouble, while in cases of severe headache a handful of leaves spread on the brow usually alleviates the pain within minutes.

CHERVIL   Ruled by Jupiter
Anthriscus cerefolium

Chervil is a graceful herb very like parsley but more delicate in flavour. It is a hardy annual which will grow to a height of twelve or so inches in a shady, damp place. The feathery, light green leaves blush pink in the sun. The seeds can be sown at four to six week intervals from March to August to provide a succession of leaves for use in soups, salads, egg and fish dishes. It runs to seed quickly so be sure to pinch out flowers as soon as they are noticed. It dries well, however, and is particularly good for growing in a trough or pot.

When my father was in Denmark, a country he loved, he learnt to make a chervil soup: *You need stock, some carrots, poached eggs and* 1 *lb chervil. This is for* 6 *people. Add the chopped chervil to the stock, boil and simmer for* $\frac{1}{4}$ *hour, add a finely chopped carrot or two and cook until tender. A poached egg is served on each plate.*

My mother's use for chervil was to add it to dried pea soup; she stirred the chopped leaves in just before serving the soup. She also made a good potato soup: 1 *pint stock or water,* 1 *lb sliced potatoes,* 1 *chopped onion,* 1 *dessertspoon flour, a little cream and some chopped chervil, all simmered on the stove until the vegetables are soft.*

The leaves of chervil are traditionally blood cleansing and diuretic; they spring-clean the system and are said to have a stimulating effect on the glands. In fever an infusion of chervil was said to increase perspiration so that the temperature was lowered. Anyeta called it the rheumatism herb, and swore by its properties in this respect. She also said it was fine for disorders of the skin, haemorroids, or congestion in the breast of the nursing mother.

I call it the Herb of Hope. By long tradition chervil soup has been eaten on the Continent on Holy Thursday. And at one time this garden herb was called *Myrrhis minor*, for its oil had an aroma similar to myrrh, which the Magi brought as one of their gifts to the Holy Child. There is the power to bring new life in chervil, it has wonderful restorative qualities and is a little herb to rejoice over.

CAPRICORN

(The Goat)

(DECEMBER 23rd – JANUARY 20th)

Element : Earth   *Planet : Saturn*

Capricorn people are prone to colds and flu and should wrap up warmly in winter. They have several weak spots, the knees especially can be sensitive and give trouble in later life. Because Capricornians are conscientious, steady, hard-working and often modest, they do not assert themselves as often as they could and so suffer from nervous shyness, or go to the other extreme and bluster a lot! They should try to surround themselves with cheerful people, because they are sometimes liable to get depressed and pessimistic about their circumstances, when there is really no need.

Best foods for health are eggs, cheese, kale, spinach, prunes, leeks, raisins, coconut, almonds, rye, bread and fish.

Health points to watch: knees, bones, ears, teeth, a tendency to colds and chills.
Herbs for health: Comfrey, Red Beets, Sorrel, Solomon's Seal.

COMFREY   Ruled by Saturn
Symphytum officinale

Country people know this humble wayside herb by several names, including 'Knitbone', and 'Nipbone', so called because of its properties in healing fractures and joining bones. The Latin *confirmo* is possibly its derivation, 'I strengthen' or perhaps *confero*, 'I gather together', which refers to early treatment of fractures. The scientific name *Symphytum* is thought to be from the Greek *Symphyo*, 'I make whole'.

Comfrey flourishes wild by the sides of rivers or ditches, where the soil is damp, and grows to a height of one or two feet or more. The leaves are large and the whole plant is covered in short, stiff hairs. The flowers, usually white, can also be yellow or pale rust and are blooming all summer.

My father once knew a countryman many years ago whose child was threatened with consumption, but he cured her by making her suck the juice from the stems of freshly gathered comfrey.

Comfrey has for many years been prescribed for chest troubles and coughs. It's still a good remedy. Boil an ounce of the crushed root (you can buy it from any herbalist) in a pint of water for ten minutes, then add an equal quantity of milk and simmer. A wineglassful should be taken every three hours.

Modern doctors have discovered long after the ancient medicine men used comfrey to mend fractures, that the powdered root is of great value in poultice-form to heal ulcerous wounds.

My mother always said that comfrey was wonderful for curing chapped hands. She would make an infusion of the herb, mix it with a little glycerine or rose water and used it after her hands had been in water for any length of time. A little comfrey sprinkled in the bathwater is also very soothing and healing for rough, tender skin.

RED BEETS   Ruled by Saturn
(Beta) Hertensis

Beetroot is a very beneficial vegetable indeed. Herbalists used the juice in times gone by to purge the head of pain, cleanse the nose, deal with ear-ache, and indeed, toothache. If you are at all anaemic it is helpful to take some beetroot juice every day because it increases the haemoglobin in the blood, but it's not very delicious when taken by itself. So why not mix it with chives or lemon balm or some lovage – anything that will improve the taste a little.

Beetroot is also a very good remedy for liver trouble, and

although it is best known in salads, makes a very tasty hot vegetable, if served with white sauce. My mother used to make a marvellous beet salad. First she cut the beetroot into cubes, then she made a thick white sauce, took it from the heat and added an egg yolk to the mixture, into which she stirred oil and vinegar until it was the consistency and colour of mayonnaise (a little sugar can be added if you please). The final touch was chopped parsley. Smother the beet cubes in this sauce, allow to cool and you have a delicious salad.

Bortsch, the Russian beet soup, was well known to Anyeta, my grandmother, and here is her recipe: *You need a rich stock from beef bones and a pig's trotter or knuckle of veal, a carrot, a parsnip, a few tomatoes, salt, sugar and black pepper, a bay leaf, thyme and an onion with some cloves stuck in it. When it has simmered 2 hours on a low heat strain the liquid and add 5 small or 4 large grated raw beets. (They must be raw.) Replace over low heat for about 15 minutes. Serve with chopped frank-furters if you wish to add some protein, but Anyeta just served sour cream. If left to chill the soup should jell overnight, but if not, help it along with some gelatine dissolved in hot water and stirred in. Serve chilled with a spoonful of cream or soured cream and ground cloves.*

SORREL   Ruled by Venus in Capricorn
Rumex acetosa

The common sorrel is a health-giving herb which has fallen into disuse lately. Very few modern housewives know it, yet it can be presented as a vegetable, or you can make a delicious soup of it in Spring. It has a reputation for curing persistent headaches, and in the herbalist Gerarde's day, he wrote: 'The leaves of Sorrel taken in good quantitie, stamped and strained into some ale, and a posset made thereof, coole the sicke body, quench thirst and allay the heate of such as are troubled with a pestilent fever, hot ague, or any great inflammation within.'

For sorrel soup take a quarter of a pound of sorrel leaf and a small lettuce and chop fine. Put in a saucepan with a knob of butter and heat over a low flame for 10 minutes, stirring to prevent it catching. Add 1½ pints milk thickened with flour and simmer for 20 minutes. Remove from heat and season with salt, pepper and a little tarragon vinegar. For a richer soup you can add an egg yolk or two beaten up in cream at the last moment before serving.

Sorrel can be grown from seed in March/April, thinning out to one foot apart or by division of root in early Spring. The French Sorrel (*Humex scutatus*) is possibly more satisfactory for cookery purposes as it has larger leaves. The herb has a rather sour flavour when raw but can be mixed in salads to give an extra 'bite'. But remember that sorrel, blood cleansing as it is, is also rich in oxylic acid, like rhubarb, and should not be taken in too great a quantity over a long period of time.

SOLOMON'S SEAL   Ruled by Saturn
Polygonatum multiflorum

Village children know this plant with its white bell-like flowers, which bloom in May, as 'Jacob's Ladder'. It's also known as 'Lily of the Mountains', 'Many Knees' (from the Latin name many jointed) and 'Our Lady's Seal'. It grows both in gardens and wild, and is about half a yard high, its slender stem from which the little bells hang down arching gracefully. It is said it deserves its name because of a mark on the root resembling the Seal of Solomon – two triangles. The Arabs say that Solomon, who 'knew the diversities of plants and the virtue of roots, set his seal upon the root as a sign of its value to man.'

The powdered root was used in poultice-form to be applied to bruising and inflammation. The decoction was taken internally for bleeding and disorders of the lungs, and the leaves, too, were used for bruising and black eyes, as Gerarde says: 'black or blue spots, gotten by falls or woman's wilfulness in stumbling upon their hasty husbands' fists and such like'.

The baby shoots of Solomon's Seal can be boiled and eaten, dipped in butter, in the way you do asparagus; otherwise it is not really a herb for the kitchen shelf.

AQUARIUS
(The Water Carrier)

(JANUARY 21st – FEBRUARY 19th)

Element: Air   *Planets: Saturn and Uranus*

Idealistic, strong-willed, original, the typical Aquarian has many health hazards to face if he or she does not watch out for nervous tension. Aquarians like the company of other people, and seek out others, hating to be alone. Yet they really do need a little more tranquillity in life than they allow themselves. Heart, eye strain, and circulation need watching. Aquarians are healthiest on a vegetarian diet, although they frequently appreciate a gourmet meal. Celery, apples, spinach, radishes, strawberries are all excellent. Coconut, figs, few eggs and some oily fish are to be advised, too.

Health points to watch: heart, eyes, circulation, nerves, liver.
Herbs for health: Elderberry, Fumitory Mullein, Barley.

ELDERBERRY   Ruled by Venus in Aquarius
Sambucus nigra

The Romanies call this 'the beneficient tree', and say that every part of it is of benefit to man, yet there is an old folk tale that if a child or young animal is struck by an elder bough in anger it will never grow any more. The common name comes from the Anglo-Saxon word *aeld* meaning 'kindle' for in early times the hollow stems of elder were used to blow through to put life into a fire.

The elder tree is beloved of the Romanies as I say, and respected by herbalists down the centuries. One wrote that

he never passed the elder tree without lifting his hat in grati-
tude to God for giving so great a blessing to mankind.

The Romanies have long known that an infusion of elder
flowers taken last thing at night soothes the spirit, induces
sleep and calms the nerves. It is also a good diuretic and
Culpeper advised that the young buds, eaten in salads in the
Spring, acted as an emetic. Elderflower water has many uses
– as an astringent for oily skin on the face, as an eye lotion, as
a mouth wash.

You can buy commercially produced elderflower water,
but if you are lucky enough to know an elder tree, gather a
handful of the flowers on a dry and sunny day, put into a jug
and cover with a pint of boiling water. Leave for twenty-
four hours and then strain. For a good astringent lotion for
the skin, mix in the juice of one lemon, but omit this if you
are using the water for an eye lotion.

My grandmother used to make a very good elderflower
cream for cosmetic use and this was her recipe: *Pick off the
petals and put into a jar with ½ oz spermaceti, ½ oz white
wax, and 8 oz olive oil. Set in a pan of water, and, while
bringing the water to the boil, stir the mixture from time to
time. Let it simmer for 1 hour, then set on one side to cool
and set.* She used to leave the petals in the cream, but they
can be strained away if desired, before the cream is set.

My father's elderberry wine was extremely heady. What
you might call a fortified wine, although he referred to it as
'cordial'. I do not recommend it for any innocent drinker,
but here is the recipe: *Strip 7 lb elderberries from their
stalks, put into a big pan, pour over them 3 gallons boiling
water. Leave for 2 days, then bruise the fruit thoroughly and
strain through a jelly bag, hair sieve, or piece of muslin.
Measure the amount of liquid obtained and put into a preserving pan with 3 lb loaf sugar, 1 lb unstoned raisins, ¼ oz
ground ginger, and 6 cloves to each gallon. Boil gently for 1
hour, skimming as needed. Draw from heat, let stand until
nearly cold, then stir in brewer's yeast in the proportion of 1
teaspoon to each gallon. Turn into a dry cask, cover the
bunghole with a cloth and leave for a fortnight. Add a wineglassful of brandy to each gallon, bung down tightly and*

leave for 6 months when the wine should be drawn off, bottled and corked.

He would serve the wine warmed on winter nights with a little ground ginger and tell me that it prevented colds and influenza – I must say that it made him very merry and he never suffered from these tedious complaints at all.

FUMITORY   Ruled by Saturn
Fumaria officinalis

Fumitory grows in almost every cultivated field and hedgerow in Britain and you may see it blossom from May to September. Anyeta used to tell village girls who were worried about superfluous hair: 'If the hairs are pulled out one or two at a time, and the place rubbed with the juice of a freshly gathered sprig of fumitory, no other hair will grow in the same place.' While the herbalist Gerarde declared that if the juice of the herb and of dock leaves were mingled with vinegar and the places gently washed therewith, it would cure all sorts of scabs, pimples, blotches, wheals on the face and hands or any other part of the body.

The plant, known as Earth Smoke, Horned Poppy, or Wax Dolls, in many parts of the country, has finely divided leaves of a whiteish shade, and small rose-coloured flowers tipped with purple.

Country folk used to drink whey infused with fumitory and any gipsy girl with a dark and oily complexion knew all about the cosmetic qualities of the herb, mixed with whey, to clear up skin troubles, just as her sister gorgio with a very fair skin trusted fumitory to remove her freckles.

Fumitory tea can be made from the leaves if picked between May and July, and then dried. The tea is fine for liver and gall bladder problems, and to cure mild depression.

MULLEIN   Ruled by Saturn
Verbascum thapsus

Aaron's rod, as it's better known to British gipsies and country people, is a familiar sight on wild, untended ground with its tall flowering spike of yellow flowers, and its woolly or hairy leaves.

The reason for it being called Aaron's Rod is plain for its flowers do indeed look like a flaming staff, but 'Mullein' is more difficult to pinpoint and it may be that it comes from the Old English 'wolleyn' meaning woollen.

Culpeper wrote: 'The decoction, if drunk, is profitable for those that are bursten, and for cramps, convulsions and old coughs. The decoction gargled, eases toothache and the oil made by infusion of the flowers, is of good effect for the piles.'

In olden times the herb was used to cure cattle of a lung complaint. It is rich in iron and magnesium.

BARLEY   Ruled by Saturn
Hordeum Vulgare

'Shut up and eat your barley soup', said the mother of a famous star in the days when he was a ten-year-old chatterbox living in a tenement in the Bronx. The Swartz family were certainly not rich, yet their nutrition was excellent for, knowingly or unknowingly, the mother of Tony Curtis fed her family well – so he tells me.

Barley is full of magnesium and nowadays people who find their nails and hair are brittle and their nerves bad, who get the cramps or sweating or dizzy fits, would do well to have more of it in their diet, either in their soup, as barley water, or in the form of good old fashioned barley pudding.

To make barley water take 3 oz pearl barley, wash in cold water, then put into a saucepan with 1 pint water, bring quickly to the boil, strain at once, then throw the water away. Now put the scalded and bleached barley into a saucepan with 2 quarts water and, having brought it to the boil, simmer until the quanity is reduced to 1 quart. Strain and pour the water over a slice of lemon, add a little sugar and the drink is ready and may be taken hot or cold.

In many cases of kidney trouble its efficiency is increased if an ounce of gum arabic is added after straining.

For constipation, add the following after the scalding: two

chopped figs and a handful of raisins, together with half an ounce of liquorice root. Proceed as before.

Don't throw away the strained barley – it will make a nourishing pudding with milk, some sugar, and an egg added, baked in the oven.

PISCES

(The Fishes)

(FEBRUARY 20th – MARCH 20th)

Element : Water   *Planets : Jupiter and Neptune*

Intensely sympathetic, sensitive, perceptive, and often brilliant, the typical Pisces subject is liable to create illness through worry. One of the most important of your rules is to try to keep your feet warm and dry, for many Pisceans suffer with some form of foot trouble or another, and can also be badly troubled by rheumatism.

Foods to maintain health are green leafy vegetables, spinach, lettuce, raisins, dates, figs and nuts, fresh fruit and root vegetables, cucumbers, beans, strawberries.

Health points to watch: chest, rheumatism, feet.
Herbs for health: Bilberries, Meadow sweet, Rose hips, Lungwort.

BILBERRIES (or Whortleberries)   Ruled by Jupiter
Vaccinium Myrtillus

This is indeed a delicious fruit and I remember well the lovely luxury of gathering them, my fingers and lips stained with the purple juice, when I was very young. The little bush, which prefers heathland and grows wild along hillsides, is about the right height for a harvesting child.

Bilberry, it's thought, comes from the Danish *böllebär,* 'dark berry', whilst 'whortleberry' may come from *myrtillus,* the Latin for an imported similar fruit of the Medieval times, which was used in medicines.

My family's recipe for bilberry cordial is as follows: *Pick* 4 *or 5 handfuls of the ripe fruit, wash, and put into ordinary wine bottles; bottle should be at least ¾ full. Fill up with good brandy, cork tightly and put away for use. The longer the cordial is kept the better it will be.*

In cases of diarrhoea a tablespoonful of this cordial given in warm water and repeated if need be every two hours, will cure when other methods have failed. By the way, the fresh juice alone is soothing on burns and scalds and will cure some forms of eczema. And hot, diluted bilberry juice, with the addition of some honey, helps coughs, colds and chest complaints.

We used to gather the young leaves of the Bilberry bush in May and dry them in a slow oven to make tea. If you are lucky enough to live near the bilberry – for it is very scarce in the countryside – it will surprise you in its likeness to household tea, because it contains a great deal of tannin. The tea has a regulating effect on the glandular system and is helpful in slimming.

MEADOWSWEET   Ruled by Jupiter
Spiraea ulmaria

There is something very English about the sight of the white heads of meadowsweet growing in their favourite place – by streams and rivers, and in damp meadows. The name is said to be corruption of the Anglo-Saxon *mede*, or *medo-wyrt* – 'mead' or 'honey-herb'.

The flowers of the meadowsweet contain iron and magnesium and, if you need these elements in your diet, I suggest you take night and morning a wineglassful of the infusion of one ounce to one pint. (You can buy the dried herb from a good herbalist.)

Culpeper tells us that the flowers are 'astringent, binding and useful in fluxes ... An infusion of the fresh-gathered tops promotes sweating ... A water distilled from the flowers is good for inflammation of the eyes.'

My mother added meadowsweet flowers and leaves to her pot-pourri mixture, and it was said to be the favourite scent of Queen Elizabeth I.

ROSE HIP
Rosa canina

Ruled by Jupiter

Rose hips have many and varied uses in herbal medicine, they are full of acidity, good for coughs and chest trouble, and are astringent in action.

Rose hips are known by modern nutritionists and scientists to be a very rich source of vitamin C and also contain vitamins A, B, E and P. We never let an Autumn go by without harvesting these valuable jewels when I was young, and I can see them now – the beautiful red hips on bare prickly stems, where the fragile pink dog roses had bloomed in Summer, seen against a glittering backdrop of hoar frost, or shimmering morning dew, according to the weather.

Because the rose hip is so rich as a nutritional source, the tea, made from the dried pips and husks is a fine preventative medicine: *Top and tail first, take 2 tablespoons of pips and husks equally, soak the hips for 12 hours in water then boil 3 pints of water in an enamel saucepan – add the hips and simmer for ½ hour, then strain.* You can keep the tea for several days in the fridge. Anyone with troublesome kidneys, especially if this shows in puffiness under the eyes, should take rose hip tea daily.

One of Anyeta's favourite remedies for banishing freckles or driving away age liver spots was a paste made up of powdered rose hips. This she spread over the affected area and left until dry – then removed with some rosewater or cucumber juice. Rose hips are also good internally for the problem of age spots, as they are known, for these are said to be due to a lack of vitamins C and E, of which rose hips are a plentiful source.

LUNGWORT
Pulmonaria officinalis

Ruled by Jupiter

Lungwort is an easily recognisable little plant with its spotted leaves and violet blue flower, and has a relative, a lichen or moss (Sticta pulmonaria). Both were always held in great esteem, for chestiness and coughs and sneezes. Indeed, in days gone by both its common and its generic names refer to its medicinal purpose. In Latin, *pulmonaria* relates to *pulmo*, 'lung' and the specific term *officinalis* 'of the shop' certainly means that it was a herb which could be acquired of any herbalist.

The dried herb can still be obtained today and may be used in the remedial treatment of coughs, lung complaints, asthma. It takes away inflammation, deals with phlegm and helps to ease wheezing breath. An infusion of one ounce to one pint of boiling water is the usual remedy, taken in as one wineglassful every two hours.

Truly one of the most valuable herbs in herbal medicine, lungwort will often work on a persistent cough where all else has failed.

The Zodiac and Herbs

Now we have come full circle, naming some of the herbs which are ruled by the Planets and Signs of Astrology, as my father taught me. There are many more, and I give their rulings and their uses on the following pages.

But before we part, let me wish you *'Kooshti Sante'* with all my heart. If you have been feeling low, of course you will have consulted your doctor – the *mulledmushengro* as we Romanies call him – the Dead-man maker – but that was an unworthy thing to say about some of the most wonderul people in our modern world. However, remember that modern drugs are really emergency measures. So often we do not elicit our doctor's help until it is too late and he is dealing with the end product – a serious disease. By the Romany way, with herbs and a good diet, we learn to live as nature intended – using the herbs and the goodness of the earth to cure our bodies, which are of the earth.

And the role of Astrology in this – is it questionable? I leave that to your judgment. Having read about your Sun-Sign its health hazards, its needs – can you deny that Astrology does not pin-point your weak spots with accuracy and assign the remedies according to its lore with mystic skill?

'And God said: Behold I have given you every herb bearing seed, which is upon the face of all the earth, and every tree in the which is the fruit of a tree yielding seed; to you it shall be for meat.' (Genesis 1 : 29).

How to Use Dried Herbs

METHOD	PART OF HERB	AMOUNT	LIQUID	TIME
Infusion	cut leaves, flowers, herbs	2 tbsp.	pour over 1 pint boiling water	10 minutes
Decoction	bark, chips, roots, seeds	2 tbsp.	boil in 1 pint water; cover pot	20 minutes

There may be some confusion as to exactly how herbs should be used for health, apart from using certain culinary herbs in cookery recipes. Above I describe the two main methods of taking medicinal herbs internally.

Infusion: Do not boil the leaves or flowers, just pour over boiling water as if you were making tea and let it steep. Fifteen minutes is the minimum, the longer you allow the herb to steep the stronger its properties available in the water. Keep the pot covered – don't use aluminium or teflon – china or stainless steel or pyrex are best. Strain the liquid into a jug before use.

Decoction: You will need to boil the herbs, barks, roots, seed or chips for at least thirty minutes. Use the same types of container as for infusion (heat proof, of course) and keep the pot covered.

Glossary of Medical Terms

ALTERATIVE   A vague term to indicate a substance which hastens the renewal of the tissues so that they can to better advantage carry on their functions.

ANODYNE   Pain-easing.

ANTHELMINTIC   Causing death or removal of worms in the body.

ANTIBILIOUS   Against biliousness.

ANTIPERIODIC   Preventing the return of those diseases which recur, such as Malaria.

ANTISCORBUTIC   Preventing Scurvy.

ANTISCROFULOUS   Preventing or curing scrofulous diseases.

ANTISEPTIC   Preventing putrefaction.

ANTISPASMODIC   Preventing or curing spasms.

APERIENT   Producing a natural movement of the bowels.

APHRODISIAC   Exciting the sexual organs.

AROMATIC   Having an aroma.

ASTRINGENT   Binding. Causing contraction of the tissues.

BALSAMIC   Of the nature of a balsam. Usually applied to substances containing resins and benzoic acid.

BITTER   Applied to bitter tasting drugs which are used to stimulate the appetite.

CARDIAC   Products which have an effect upon the heart.

CARMINATIVE   Easing griping pains and expelling flatulence.

CATHARTIC   Producing evacuation of the bowels.

CHOLAGOGUE   Producing a flow of bile.

CORRECTIVE   Restoring to a healthy state.

DEMULCENT   Applied to drugs which sooth and protect the alimentary canal.

DEOBSTRUENT   Clearing away obstructions by opening the natural passages of the body.

DEPURATIVE   A purifying agent.

DERMATIC   Applied to drugs with an action on the skin.

DETERGENT   Cleansing.

DIAPHORETIC   Drugs which promote perspiration.

DIGESTIVE   Aiding digestion.

EMETIC   Applied to drugs which cause vomiting.

EMMENAGOGUE   Applied to drugs which have the power of exciting the menstrual discharge.

EMOLLIENT   Used in relation to substances which have a softening and soothing effect.

EXPECTORANT   Promoting expectoration and removing secretions from the bronchial tubes.

FEBRIFUGE   Reducing fever.

HAEMOSTATIC   Drugs used to control bleeding.

HEPATIC   Used in connection with substances having an effect upon the liver.

HYDROGUE   Having the property of removing accumulations of water or serum. Causing watery evacuations.

HYPNOTIC   Producing sleep.

INSECTICIDE   Having the property of killing insects.

IRRITANT   Causing irritation.

LAXATIVE   A gentle bowel stimulant.

MYDRIATIC   Causing dilation of the pupil.

MYOTIC   Contracting the pupil.

NARCOTIC   Applied to drugs producing stupor and insensibility.

NEPHRITIC   Drugs having an action upon the kidneys.

NERVINE   Applied to drugs used to restore the nerves to their natural state.

NUTRITIVE   Nourishing.

OXYTOCIC   Hastening birth by stimulating the contraction of the uterus.

PARASITICIDE   Destroying parasites.

PARURIENT   Applied to substances used during childbirth.

PECTORAL Used in connection with drugs used internally for affections of the chest and lungs.

PURGATIVE Drugs which evacuate the bowels. More drastic than a laxative or aperient.

REFRIGERANT Relieving thirst and giving a feeling of coolness.

RESOLVENT A term used to denote substances applied to swellings in order to reduce them.

RUBEFACIENT Applied to counter-irritants. Substances which produce blisters or inflammation.

SEDATIVE Drugs which calm nervous excitement.

STERNUTATORY Producing sneezing by irritation of the mucous membrane.

STIMULANT Energy producing.

STOMACHIC Applied to drugs for disorders of the stomach.

STYPTIC Substances which clot the blood and thus stop bleeding.

SUDORIFIC Producing copious perspiration.

TAENIACIDE Applied to drugs used to expel tape-worm.

TONIC Substances which give tone to the body producing a feeling of well being.

VERMIFUGE Substances which expel worms form the body.

VULNERARY Used in healing wounds.

Books in the Living with Herbs Series

An open-end series of beautiful paperbacks you can use in so many practical ways — written by leading herbalists and herb marketers. Each book contains four pages of full-color illustration, and many black and white drawings. Each volume is $2.50 per copy and they also come packaged in a 4-volume set ($10.00) for holiday gifts. Four titles in print now, with more to come.

At your nearest book, herbal supply or health store, or order direct from the publisher (postpaid).

Vol. 1 **Herbs, Health and Astrology**
by Leon Petulengro

A famous gypsy and noted astrologer records some of the ancient Romany beliefs about herbs and their links with astrology. Health patterns found in each of the Signs are discussed and the author offers specific remedies for various ailments based on *herbal astrological confluence.* Mr. Petulengro devotes an entire chapter to each Zodiac sign and a description of how the planets rule herbs. Includes many unusual recipes. $2.50

Vol. 2 **Choosing, Planting and Cultivating Herbs**
by Philippa Back

Herbs for city and country dweller, for gardeners who plan whole herb gardens and for those who may want to grow herbs in more modest surroundings — in window boxes, on balconies, in pots hung on trellises, or for other indoor pleasure. Philippa Back co-authored the famed *Herbs for Health* with Claire Loewenfeld. She includes an alphabetical listing of herbs as well as many garden plans and herb drawings. $2.50

Vol. 3 **Growing Herbs as Aromatics**
by Roy Genders

Here is told the history of pomanders, potpourris, scented waters, hanging baskets, rose perfumes and other uses of aromatics and spices. Best of all, the author shows how they can be grown and harvested, and includes a variety of ideas and recipes for their use today. Roy Genders' books include *A History of Scent, The Cottage Guide,* and *Scented Wild Flowers of Britain.* $2.50

Vol. 4 **Making Things with Herbs**
by Elizabeth Walker

Professional help for using herbs to make gifts, practical and frivolous, to adorn and embellish the house. Sachets, sweet bags, herbal teas, herbal essences, herb sacks for the kitchen, toys stuffed with herbs, and all kinds of other delights become so easy with Ms. Walker's practical expert advice. The author's experience comes from running a very active family business called "Meadow Herbs" in England, which makes and markets herb products. $2.50

The *Living with Herbs* Series is published by
Keats Publishing, Inc., New Canaan, Connecticut, 06840.